INTERNATIONAL PEACE GARDEN

promise of peace

Photography by Kari L. Barchenger

Flowers appear on the earth; the season of singing has come, the cooing of doves is heard in our land. - Song of Solomon 2:12

Acknowledgment

This book would not have been possible if I had not gone with my dad Arthur Norby, to deliver the newest sculpture "Promise of Peace" to the Peace Garden in August of 2015. While we were in the gift shop, we saw that there was not a book available about the Peace Garden. While discussing this omission we learned there had never been a book produced showing the beauty of the Peace Garden. With that insight I have endeavored to capture a small part of that beauty in this first ever photography collection of the International Peace Garden.

All the images in this book were taken in 2015 and 2016

I would like to thank Garry Enns, CEO of the International Peace Garden for providing the Foreward to this book.

Thanks to Vern Zink of the WBCCI, and Arthur Norby for writing the content about the sculpture "Promise of Peace".

Thanks to my dad, Arthur Norby and his wife, Kathy Spangler-Norby for helping me with the content and layout of the book.
For being at the other end of the phone to answer my questions and advise me.

I would also like to thank Johannes and Connie from the International Peace Garden,
Don Kinzler, horticulturist, Neal & Adam from Sheyenne Gardens in Harwood ND for helping me identify the plants in the Peace Garden

Foreword

The International Peace Garden is built on a promise of peace. Its founders chose to locate this garden of peace in the heart of the Turtle Mountains, in the centre of this great continent we call North America; also known as Turtle Island among the indigenous peoples on this land.

The indigenous people of this region understood the importance of the Turtle Mountains as a meeting place and as a central meeting place in a trading network stretching from what we now know as South Dakota in the south to Hudson's Bay in the north. At one time, as glacial ice made its retreat north and Glacial Lakes Agassiz to the east and Souris to the west of the Turtle Mountains were formed, the ridge of glacial deposits stretching from north to south made it possible for the First People on Turtle Island to begin exploring this newly uncovered land.

The original vision of the International Peace Garden grew from discussions among international horticulturists and gardeners at gatherings in Toronto and New York. The time was the late 1920's and the hope for a continued peace following "the war to end all wars" was more than a dream. The reality of the Great Depression and the rise of fascism in Europe did not dampen the spirits of the more than 50,000 people who came to dedicate the International Peace Garden on July 14, 1932.

The Cairn, which still stands at the entrance to the International Peace Garden, was dedicated that day to mark the enduring peace that exists between our two great nations – United States of America and Canada. The cairn's plaque, in part, affirms that "We two nations dedicate this garden and pledge ourselves that as long as men shall live we will not take up arms against one another."

The International Peace Garden's 2,300 acres is nestled in the heart of the Turtle Mountains right on the 49th parallel. Central to the Garden is a 25-acre formal garden with brilliant flower beds that invite all its visitors to stop for a while, to enjoy the beauty of thousands of flowers, and to imagine a world where all nations could be at peace with one another.

This commemorative book offers you a glimpse at the treasure that is the International Peace Garden. It invites you to come to "the Garden" and experience a "Promise of Peace" as exemplified by a new installation in the centre of our Formal Garden fountain. It helps bring to life the hope we all share of a world without war and the fear and misery that grows out of war. It helps rekindle the hope expressed in the original constitution of the International Peace Garden and shared by the thousands who attended the International Peace Garden's official opening:

"The purpose of the organization is to foster and give protection and support to the material expression of a world ideal concerned in the interest of International Peace and its benefits to humanity.

"It recognizes that wars between nations have been humanity's greatest curse; that its glories are a myth; and its continuance an abhorrence to the Creator….."

The photographs in this collection were taken by Kari Barchenger in the summer of 2015. She had never been to the International Peace Garden prior to accompanying her father Arthur Norby to the Garden the day he delivered his sculpture, created for the International Peace Garden, which is called "a Promise of Peace". The Wally Byam Caravan Club International – WBBCI - sponsored the creation and casting of the sculpture to replace one which had not withstood the test of time. The hands and dove sit in the center of the Formal Garden fountain as a commitment to the ideals of the Garden's founders and current members and supporters.

Kari was overwhelmed by the beauty of our gardens and – as a professional photographer – recognized the need for a collection of photographs that would carry a promise of peace beyond the boundaries of the international Peace Garden. The collection you hold is the first of its kind. We know it will not be the last. Kari is already planning her summer to include regular excursions to the International Peace Garden.

She plans to build on this collection of images, including seasonal photographs. Those of us who work at the Garden experience the fall, winter, and spring beauty of this special place. It is our hope that you will consider exploring our promise of peace in all seasons.

This collection of amazing photographs is just a small representation of what can be found at the International Peace Garden. Kari has chosen the best of the more than 100,000 flowers we planted in 2015. The designs of the flower beds change every year, which means there is something new for you to see every day and from year to year.

Enjoy this collection. And enjoy our Garden.

And, thank you Kari.

Sincerely,

Garry Enns, CEO
International Peace Garden

To God in His Glory,

We two nations dedicate this garden, and pledge ourselves that as long as men shall live, we will not take up arms against one another.

This is the inscription on the Cairn found at the entrance of the garden and that was dedicated in 1932

Interpretive Center, Conservatory & Sunken Garden

The Interpretive Center & Conservatory houses the Cacti & Succulent Gardens and is open year round.

The Reflection Pool is located in the center of the Sunken Garden surrounded by thousands of perennials and annuals.

Promise of Peace

The sculpture, which represents the continuing peace between the United States and Canada is located on the 49th parallel facing west, at the east end of the garden in a fountain,

This is the most recent addition to the garden and was dedicated on July 24, 2016.

The Promise of Peace sculpture will be permanently installed in the Formal Garden Fountain

North Fountain, Sunken Garden

Stone Shelter, Sunken Garden

Peace Tower - There are four columns that are 120 feet tall.

The formal garden is located on 25 acres within the 2,300 acre Garden

Carillon Bell Tower, with 14 Arma Sifton bells which chime on the quarter-hour.

Floral Clock

Two to three thousand annuals are used in the design of the Floral Clock, which has a new design each year.

Peace Poles - Each side of the poles say "May Peace Prevail" in a different language.

Formal Garden

Top Terrace, Formal Garden

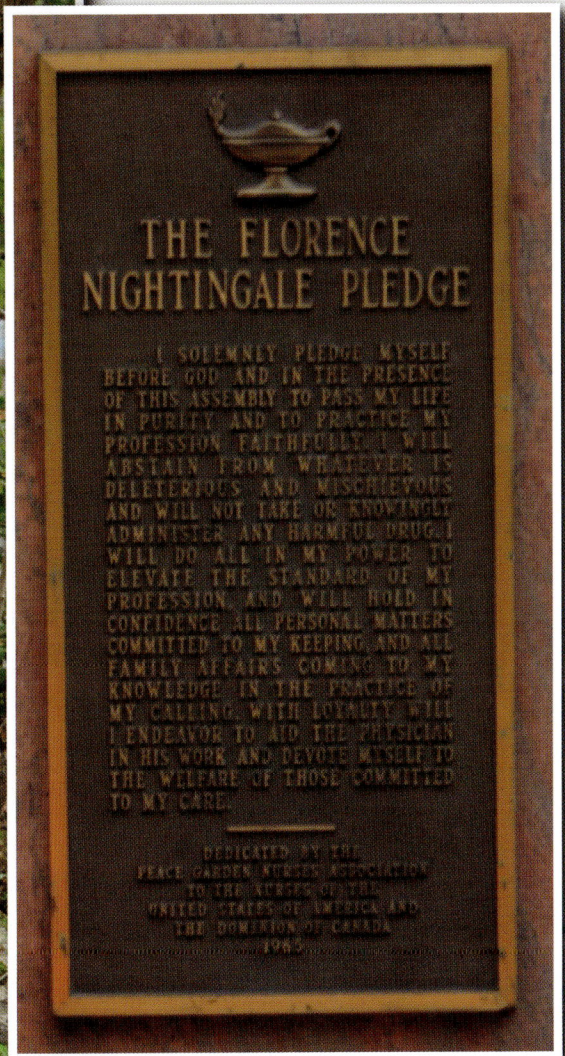

THE FLORENCE NIGHTINGALE PLEDGE

I SOLEMNLY PLEDGE MYSELF BEFORE GOD AND IN THE PRESENCE OF THIS ASSEMBLY TO PASS MY LIFE IN PURITY AND TO PRACTICE MY PROFESSION FAITHFULLY. I WILL ABSTAIN FROM WHATEVER IS DELETERIOUS AND MISCHIEVOUS AND WILL NOT TAKE OR KNOWINGLY ADMINISTER ANY HARMFUL DRUG. I WILL DO ALL IN MY POWER TO ELEVATE THE STANDARD OF MY PROFESSION, AND WILL HOLD IN CONFIDENCE ALL PERSONAL MATTERS COMMITTED TO MY KEEPING, AND ALL FAMILY AFFAIRS COMING TO MY KNOWLEDGE IN THE PRACTICE OF MY CALLING. WITH LOYALTY WILL I ENDEAVOR TO AID THE PHYSICIAN IN HIS WORK AND DEVOTE MYSELF TO THE WELFARE OF THOSE COMMITTED TO MY CARE.

DEDICATED BY THE PEACE GARDEN NURSES ASSOCIATION TO THE NURSES OF THE UNITED STATES OF AMERICA AND THE DOMINION OF CANADA 1965

Nurse's Plaque

19

Quentin Burdick Performing Arts Center

Located at the International Music Camp, it contains a state of the art concert hall that has seating for 510 and has some of the best acoustics in the area.

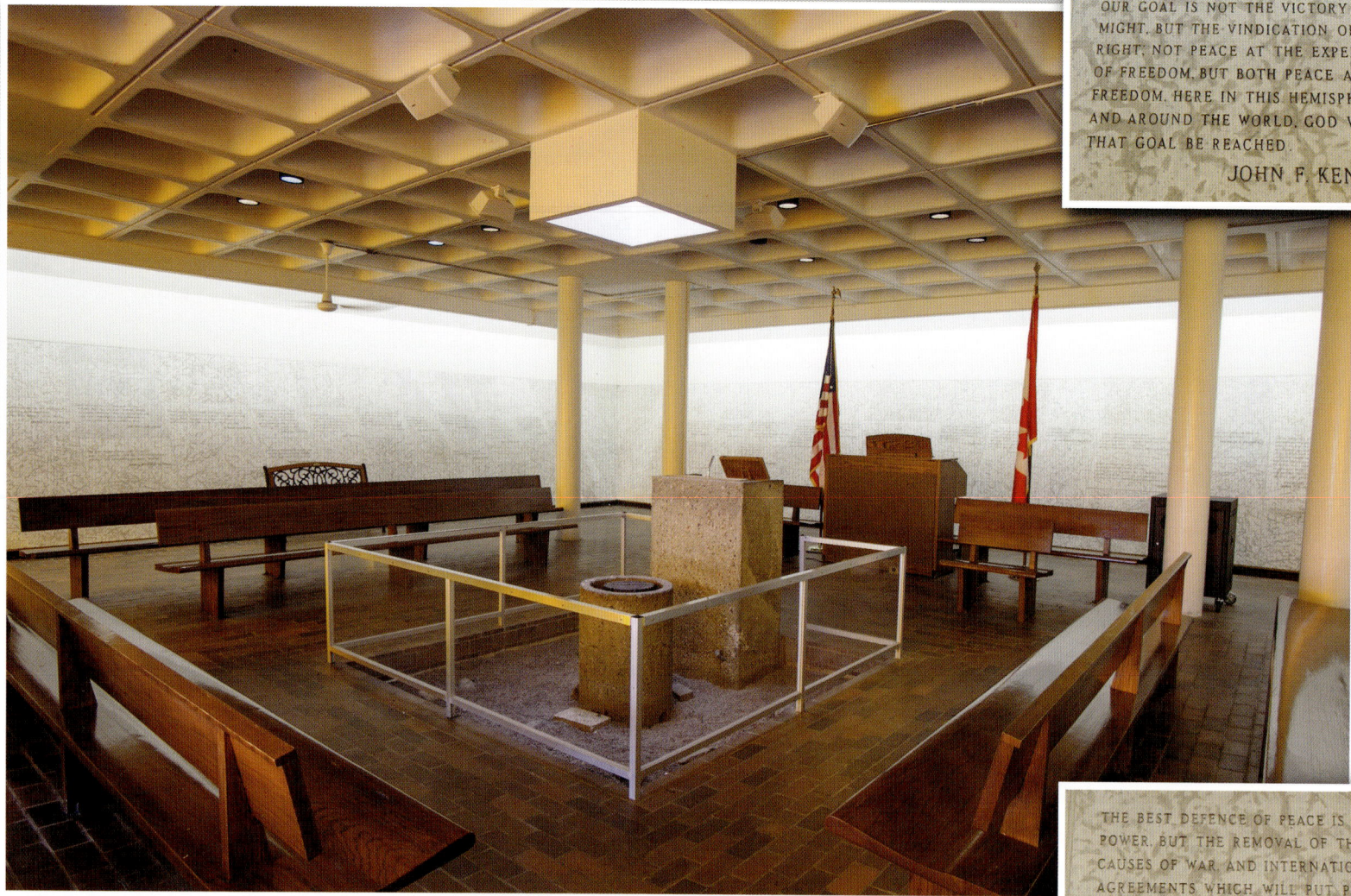

OUR GOAL IS NOT THE VICTORY OF MIGHT, BUT THE VINDICATION OF RIGHT; NOT PEACE AT THE EXPENSE OF FREEDOM, BUT BOTH PEACE AND FREEDOM, HERE IN THIS HEMISPHERE AND AROUND THE WORLD, GOD WILLING THAT GOAL BE REACHED.

JOHN F. KENNEDY

THE BEST DEFENCE OF PEACE IS NOT POWER, BUT THE REMOVAL OF THE CAUSES OF WAR, AND INTERNATIONAL AGREEMENTS WHICH WILL PUT PEACE ON A STRONGER FOUNDATION THAN THE TERROR OF DESTRUCTION

HON LESTER B PEARSON

Peace Chapel

Located at the West end of the garden, the chapel contains numerous inscriptions about peace on the interior walls.

Historic Lodge

The lodge was built in the 1930's and is the oldest building at the International Peace Garden.
The foundation is made of granite from North Dakota. The timbers are from the Duck Mountains in Manitoba.

In 2008, this lodge was added to the National Register of Historic Places in the United States.

The Gardens

The park encompasses 3.65-square-miles (9.5 km2) and 2,339 acres.

There are over 75,000 flowering shrubs, perennials and bulbs in the border garden design, along with roughly 150,000 annuals that are planted each year throughout the rest of the gardens.

Sunken Garden

Leucanthemum x superbum Shasta Daisy

Petunia 'Pink wave'   Pink Wave Petunia

Cosmos 'Double click cranberry'

Cosmos 'Double Click Cranberry'
Cranberry"Cranberry"

Echinacea purpurea 'Magnus'   Purple Coneflower

Sunken Garden, North Fountain

Canna indica 'Phasion'   Canna

Sunken Garden

Rudbeckia hirta 'Denver Daisy' Black-eyed Susan

Rudbeckia hirta 'Indian Summer' Black-eyed Susan

With over 150,000 annuals and perennials the appearance of the gardens are always changing due to the timing of the blossoms.

Rudbeckia hirta 'Cappuccino' Black-eyed Susan

Phlox paniculata 'David'   Garden Phlox

Calamagrostis 'Karl Foerster'   Feather-reed grass

Rosa 'Peace Garden' Peace Garden Rose

Petunia and Black-eyed Susan

Veronica zp.   Speedwell

Cosmos 'Double click cranberry'

Cosmos 'Double click bonbon'

Cosmos 'Sensation Picotee'

Pennisetum setaceum 'Rubrum' Fountain Grass

Hemerocallis 'Hyperion' Daylily

Cabbage White Butterfly
Veronica zp. Speedwell

Hemerocallis 'Hyperion' Daylily

Physostegia virginiana   Obedient Plant

Sempervivum sp.   Hens and Chicks

Salvia farinacea 'Rhea'   Mealy blue Sage

Hosta 'Sum and Substance'

Peacock Sculpture

The Courtyard

Rosa 'Adelaide Hoodless' Adelaide Hoodless Rose

The Courtyard

Vitko Xeric Collection

The Vitko Xeric collection was donated in 2010, to the International Peace Garden by Don and Kim Vitko of Minot, North Dakota.

Don Vitko spent 45 years passionately tending his collection of rare and amazing plants.

The Vitko Xeric Collection contains nearly 6500 cacti, succulents and other xerophytes. It is housed in a 10,000 square foot conservatory and is one of the most extensive indoor cactus and succulent collections in North America.

Tropical Walkway

Schlumbergera sp.   Christmas Cactus

Gymnocalycium horstii Chin cactus

Phaleanopsis hybrid   Orchid

Pilosocereus sp. Tree cactus

Haworthia cuspidata Pinwheel plant

Queen Victoria Agave

This Queen Victoria Agave blooms approximately every 30 years. It last bloomed in 2015.

Agave victoriae-reginae   Queen Victoria's Agave

Echeveria cultivar   Mexican Hens and Chicks

Adenium sp.   Desert Rose

Myrtillocactus geometrizens cristata   Crested Myrtillocactus

Agava sp. Century Plant

Mammillaria magnifica   Pincushion cactus

Natocactus magnificus   Chin cactus

Echeveria sp.   Mexican Hens and Chicks

Echeveria hybrid   Mexican Hens and Chicks

North American Collection

South American Collection

African Collection

Stenocactus sp.   Stenocactus

Senecio fulgens   Senecio

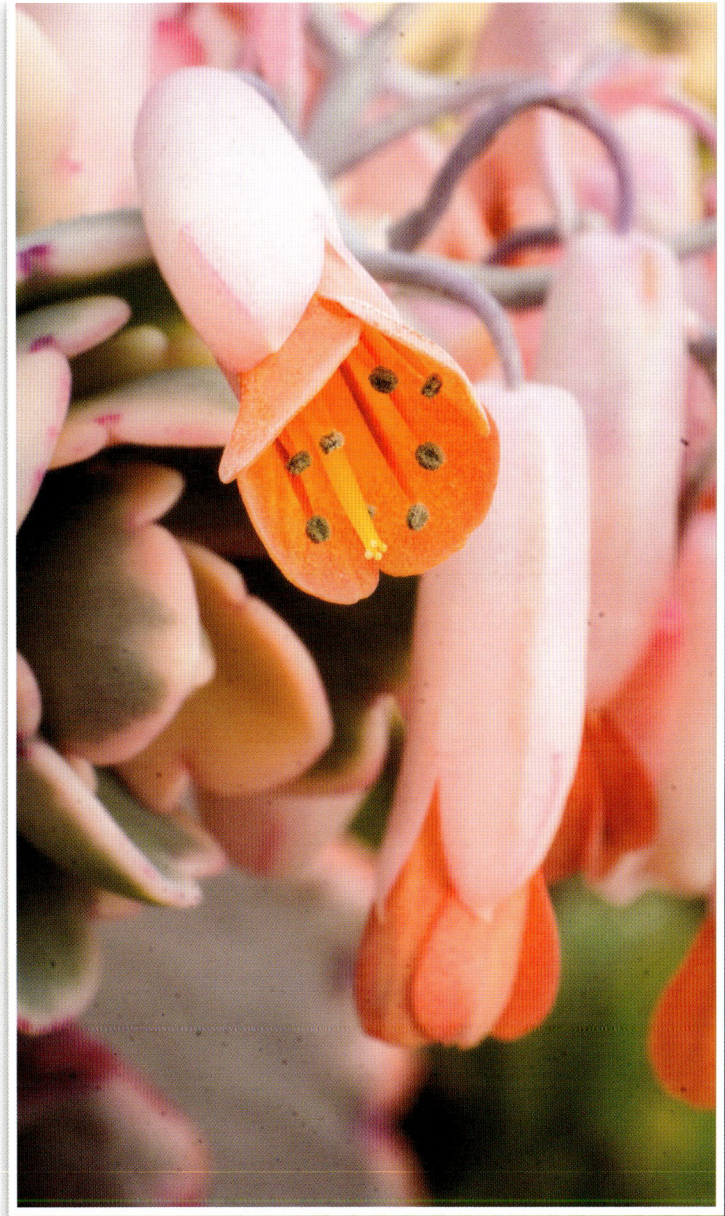

Kalanchoe fedtschenkoi variegata   Variegated lavender scallops

79

Haworthia glauca   Pinwheel plant

Haworthia turgida   Pinwheel plant

Haworthia Cassytha   Pinwheel plant

Haworthia Nigra elongata   Pinwheel plant

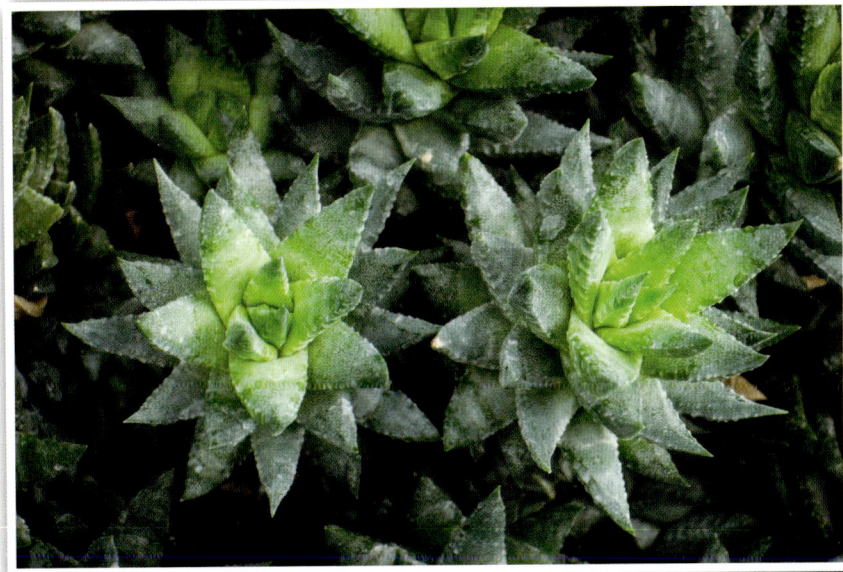

Haworthia Glauca v. jacobseniana   Pinwheel plant

Haworthia Glauca v. herrei   Pinwheel plant

Clivia miniata   Clivia/Natal Bush Lily

Lycianthes rantonnei   Potato Bush

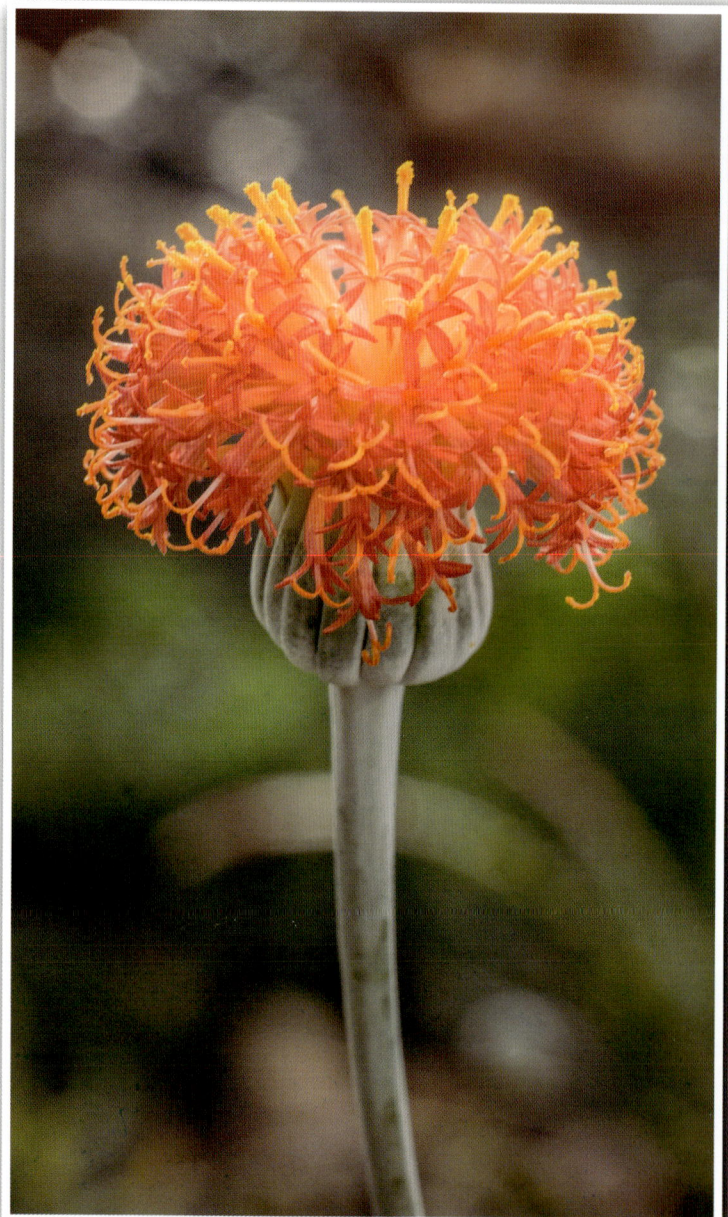

Senecio fulgens   Senecio

International Music Camp

The Music camp has youth from over 74 countries and offers programs in Music, Theater and Dance, Visual Arts & Creative Arts.
It also offers Professional Development for Educators.

internationalmusiccamp.com

International Athletic Camp

The athletic camp hosts over 1,200 athletes in 8 sports each year

Royal Canadian Legion Memorial Sports Complex

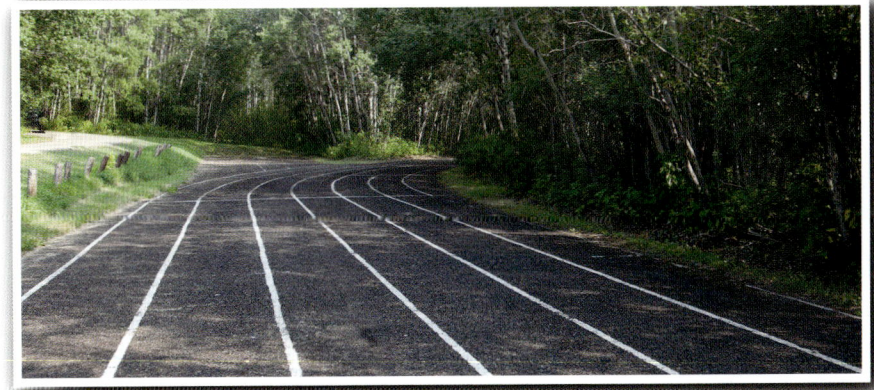

Outdoor track

www.legionathleticcamp.com

Let Peace Prevail

The International Peace Garden represents a unique and enduring symbol of the strength of our friendship as nations, our mutual respect and our shared desire for world peace.

The events of September 11, 2001 failed to shake the foundation of our shared vision of peace and prosperity for all the world's people.

This cairn, composed of steel rescued from the devastation of the World Trade Center in New York, ensures the memory of this tragedy will not be lost and reminds us to cherish tolerance, understanding and freedom.

Officially unveiled by The Honourable Gary Doer, Premier of Manitoba

September 11, 2002

911 Memorial

Steel griders from the Twin Towers in New York, NY that collapsed after being struck by terrorists on September 11, 2001, are placed to honor the firefighters who died that day.

Promise of Peace Sculpture

The history of the Promise of Peace began in 1975 when the Wally Byam Caravan Club International commissioned a small sculpture made of fiber glass and aluminum. Placed in a fountain at the International Peace Gardens, it proved to be incompatible with the water and climate, deteriorating in only a few years. It had to be removed.

It was not until 2005, that interest in sculpture was renewed when international President of WBCCI James Haddaway found no record, oral history, or photographs could be found in WBCCI records. In July, at a rally at the International Peace Gardens, the North Dakota Peace Garden Unit of WBCCI opted to take on the replacement and restoration of the sculpture. Vern Zink, then President of the North Dakota Unit presented a new plan at the Regional Rally in De Pere, Wisconsin. Then at the International Winter meeting in Hattiesburg, Mississippi a project committee was formed.

In June, 2013, Vern Zink visited the home, studio and private sculpture garden of artist Norby located in New London, Minnesota. Norby and his wife Kathyrn Spangler shared Norby's history. As an artist in 1976, Norby had promised himself one more year as an artist. That year has become forty years, during which .

Norby has created more than two dozen public sculpture including the Minnesota Korean War Veterans Memorial located at the State Capital in ST. Paul, Minnesota. Other large scale works are located from New Jersey to Arizona. In addition to these public sculptures he has created several hundred decorative sculptures, with collectors in at least eight countries of the world.

Vern Zink and his wife, Bev returned to New London in June of 2014. During that trip they were treated to view three life-sized sculptures Norby was creating for Minnesota families. Within a matter of few hours Norby and the Zinks had settled on a concept for a new fountain sculpture for the International Peace Garden. Norby explained that he was mostly retired, accepting only interesting when presented. The International Peace Garden project was exactly where his interest lie.

Although, with no written contract to rely on, Norby went to work and created a small model (called a Marquette) of the concept he and Zink had discussed. He presented that model to the Committee and others from the North Dakota Peace Garden Unit of WBCCI in Fargo, North Dakota, in September, 2014. With a go-ahead from the Committee, Norby began work on the full scale clay model. On December, 25, 2014 Norby left New London for Alpine, Utah, with three crates containing the disassembled clay sculpture. He arrived at the Adonis Art Foundry on December 30, leaving his precious cargo for mold making, casting, reassembling, and polishing. He returned in June, 2015, to retrieve the sculpture which was now cast and finished in a highly polished stainless steel. It weighs three hundred thirty pounds. When asked why he would travel sixteen hundred miles each way to complete the casting process, Norby indicated in his experience Adonis was the one art foundry he could trust with such an important project.

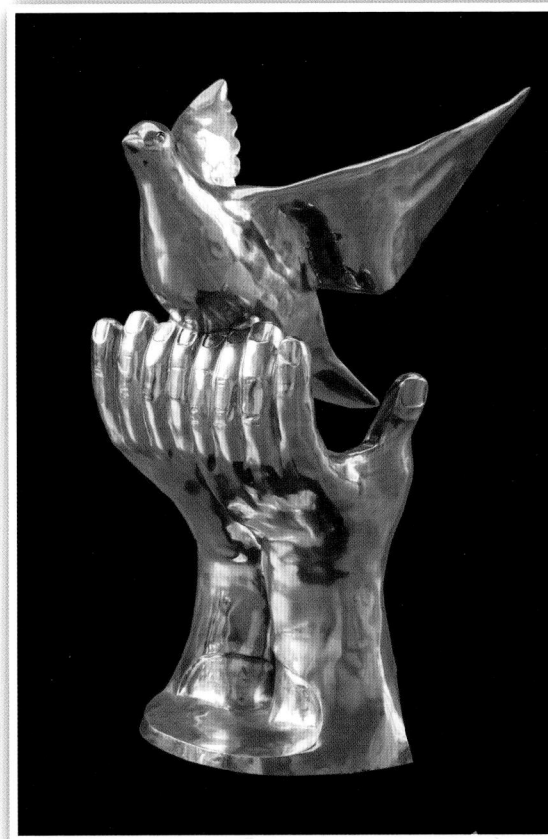

The sculpture rested at Norby's studio until August, when he delivered it to the International Peace Garden. Even as it was unloaded and temporarily placed in the Interpretive Center atrium it drew positive responses from dozens of visitors.

The Promise of Peace sculpture, cast in stainless steel, stands six feet tall. The hands which are releasing a dove are by themselves four feet tall and the bird, with wings each three feet long, is sixty inches from beak to tail. Representing the Hope of Peace, the sculpture resides on the border between Canada and the United States, with a shared message for Peace.